LIVING ON A SONG A DAY

Poems by
Rayne O'Brian

BLUE LIGHT PRESS ◆ 1ST WORLD PUBLISHING

1ST WORLD
PUBLISHING

SAN FRANCISCO ◆ FAIRFIELD ◆ DELHI

LIVING ON A SONG A DAY

BLUE LIGHT PRESS
www.bluelightpress.com
bluelightpress@aol.com

1ST WORLD PUBLISHING
PO Box 2211
Fairfield, IA 52556
www.1stworldpublishing.com

BOOK & COVER DESIGN
Melanie Gendron
melaniegendron999@gmail.com

COVER CONCEPT
Rayne O'Brian

AUTHOR PHOTO
Jason Schwager

FIRST EDITION

ISBN: 978-1-4218-3683-6

LIVING ON A SONG A DAY

Contents

Rat Pack Healer

Elsa's rings jingle on her walker
her I.V. trails a translucent snake
from a ghost garden

Where is Grand Central?
I want to go home. Take me home?

Everyone here wants to go home
No one ever will. No touch. No visits
except Frank Sinatra

You are all I long for, all I worship
and adore

Elsa believes him
Something like a blush travels her
tangled spine

God wiped her memory clean
to be ready for heaven

Frank sings, *Come fly with me*

And Elsa does
rides a currant of song to a crystal
Casino in Cassiopeia

Oh, Rat Pack healer with a bronze
swirl of bourbon in a Baccarat glass
where even jokes wore tuxedos

fly me to the moon

What is it in that voice? It says
its okay sweetheart
Wanna dance?

*One for my baby, and one more for
the road*

Who knew, Frank
This was your road

Tomb of The Wrestlers*

Tomb–Say it!
The word sings to itself doesn't it
Ooo — the musical ghost
Mmm — evermore humming

The painting of one red rose fills the room
The naked wrestlers locked
in each other's arms
but not with love

Their terrible sweat rising
to perfume the rose
Aren't we all wrestlers here
held fast in scripted embrace

When the litany of losses render
the perfumed ash of a thousand
annihilations
is this what remains
The sacred flower
and nothing else

Is that what you saw Renee

*from a painting by René Magritte

Kitchen Table

If it were not for the forest
where I was born
the logger in his high boots
who trucked me to the mill
where the carpenter built me
with his careful hands
his dowels and drills his bright saw

I would not hold this high office

Two A.M. You wept
your head heavy on your arms
Some days you butter raisin toast
and sing, turn the pages
of Whitman

Whatever you bring me I love

Walking Down Fourth Street

The day after Christmas

a red-lettered banner sashed
a fancy shop window

ANGELS — 50% OFF

When the weary night janitor
packed up the manger, all angels
lost half their value

Oh, cock-eyed world!

If the sign said, *ANGELS — FREE!*
Would shoppers stampede
knock over mannequins?

People buy angels for decoration
and receive blessings anyway

Look at it this way—

Today, a poor man can afford
his own angel—shining
above his bed

What about the old woman asleep
in the doorway's awkward embrace
a newspaper over her head

Let her rest, officer

Who knows what silver-clad warriors
she led
over snowy Alps to victory

Why Ghosts Wear Sheets

Only new ghosts wear sheets
Sheets are just training togs
The novice still clings, longs for
music, kisses and cake

You can't just die and
be a ghost right away
You gotta go to school —
be certified

First you learn to lurk
purple a shadow
sway a curtain
when no breeze blows

When you're dead six months
you can work Halloween

After a year — Advanced Pranks

You go diaphanous
Haunt Houses I and II
scent the air with jasmine or rose
Learn border etiquette for cemeteries

Refine your gift

At the highest level you are named
Messenger, and then you can enter
dreams
nudge objects

This morning on my walk
a willow branch bent low before me
scattering light at my feet

That was you, wasn't it

Ex Libris

My desire is not different than the longing
of the tides for the moon's ineluctable tug

My spine blooms at your touch, musk rose
gardenia startled with dew

Hold me

We'll ride a cranky camel over the star-kissed
Sahara. Then tuck those stars in our pockets
and toss them back up over Phoenicia
5000 BC

When we meet again after so many years
you'll find me more beautiful than when
we first met

Yes I've had other lovers. Many

But for tonight —
The stars will blink in amazement
that one of their own could know such joy

Open me

Light

Blazing like a reef of diamonds
the theory of relativity in a picture frame
hangs on a blue wall over my bed and minds
my dreams

Above the shelf of worn Teddy bears
handwritten on white cardboard, shine
the equations of Archimedes and Pythagoras

What company for a seven year old girl

The room was cool and the dawn had
not yet dressed
A yellow bulb flung a napkin of light
on the blackboard
On that darkness, with snowy chalk I wrote
the sacred equation: $e=mc^2$

My fingers tingled like almost touching
an angel. The chalk dust shivered
Then the door rasped open
Albert Einstein stepped in
A log dropped to its knees in the grate

He smiled at his equation. It quivered
like a garden creature that recognized him
His gaze turned to me. I saw the holy empire
of numbers, sorcerers' keys, in his eyes

Beloved child. Welcome

We stood together wrapped
in the apricot aroma of his pipe tobacco

He offered me his arm like I was grown
Walk with me. We'll stroll the Elbe

We'll talk about light

My Viking Blood

Does my blood leap when I kill
a tiny creature trekking the savanna
of my spinach leaf

Forgiveness is not stored in the body

Dragon ships spear the angry Atlantic
My axe exults on the gunnel

Forgiveness is a practice

We blackened the village with Eric the Red

Forgiveness is the honey of the soul

And what if on every kitchen table beside
the salt and pepper
packets of forgiveness to spread upon your
daily bread

His prison guard said Saddam Hussein
spent his last days tending a rose bush

How did it feel, Saddam, your soiled
hands helping something grow
Before your eyes were closed forever
did you see the white rose
open

Anthony Bourdain

It was not your face you saw
in the mirror at Chambord
but some hideous beast loosed
from Hades whose gaze kills
little finches and blackens
the lilies of the field

Unless you kill him

Tonight I'll serve coq au vin
paired with a local red
And set your place at my table
Life would not go hang itself

Roses Speak After Human Love

In the beginning we skinny-dipped
in the Dawn — splashing petals
in her streams — pink, gold, red

Now on earth we comfort
the fields, sweeten
the breeze with our breath
You bring us into your home
Confined in vases' crystal
clutch — or is it an embrace?

It's not that we're afraid
or haven't listened
to the stone Buddha
in the garden

We remember the wind before
it was Bach

May we share
a few last moments
Your human paradise
made us forget the sky

Such happiness we knew
at your pine table, silver-capped
salt and pepper, our faces reflect
in the toaster
the benevolence of the chandelier
spangling praise upon us

You became a rose
to speak with us

How many long afternoons you gazed
turning the vase, adoring
every change
You said, *Oh look, the yellow rose*
lifts her head, sings a cappella

But we were born with the scent
of farewell

Close your eyes

I'll go first

Things Fall Apart

Cornbread crumbles in my hand
dropping yellow pollen in
the hollows of the bacon

Fading roses escorted
to the sink, loose a path
of petals to the floor

Wait!

Don't be quick to sweep —
Once flowers sprang
everywhere the Buddha stepped

Here's the thing
Hens lay eggs
It's what they do
Things fall apart
It's what they do

Beauty wept on the battlefield
But stayed to tend the light
Goya knew

So lift your fiddle to your chin
Mourn with Lorca
Walk with Whitman

Now help me with this
what shall I wear
to dine with Baudelaire

To dance with Dante, Kabir
and Keats

still singing

Guests of the Beast

To a Delphinium

You stood as close together as daylight
will allow
A whispering distance of sibilant secrets
under blue eyelids

You are, even the lilies agree, the perfect pair
Azure hospitality. Silky cups circle your
straight-to-heaven stalks; offer remedies
for bees, high tea for a Monarch

I enter the garden, a moose with clippers
working the ground, cleaning up
One careless step back and you are dead

Snapped. Just like that
You lay there—perfect—surprised

I dropped down beside you and cry
Dear loveliest Delphinium, please forgive
this idiot. You, so vibrant, full of high purpose
I didn't know you could break like this

I place you gently beside your love
(already dazed with loss, she saw you fall)

What you release to the earth I say she will
pull up into herself. She will drink you

You will become one and, yes
I understand it is not the same

It is not ever the same

Walk as if Kissing the Earth with Your Feet. . . *

Okay. I'll do that. Step... and step...
I walk on Fourth Street past closed shops
My kiss drifts down through earth's crust
melts in the mantle, to bounce
in the hiss of the magma

Such intimacy!

Dear Earth, your intricate insects gone
the linquistic genius of bees
now they are few

Accept my condolences

We don't know how the meadowlark
reminds the stone to love the star

*— *Thich Nhat Hanh, PEACE IS EVERY STEP*

19

You Know What?

It's cold. A grey dog shivering on the damp sidewalk
A rope leash binds him to a parking meter
Nearby, a boy tugs a carpet square from his backpack
Good dog he says in a wind-chime tone and pats
the square. The dog settles down on it

At the intersection of their gaze a thousand campfires blaze

Still pretty in its plastic envelope, a Gardenia glows in the gutter
Royalty visiting the poor: crushed cups broken bottles

A street sweeper in jonquil-yellow jumpsuit rescues it
carries it to the old woman sleeping
under the merciful arch of Wells Fargo
he sets it close to her seamed face

Closer now to paradise

Who told them to make these offerings?
Is there a Great Whisperer riding the wind?
Is it the breath of Asclepius or the Sea of Galilee?

Can we make a net of light before it's too dark?

Things You Can Do

Wrap some kind words
in a warm napkin
like biscuits
and give them away

Plant a row of praise jars
on your porch
Keep fresh praise in your pantry
by the butter and jam

Rinse your words in moonlight
Braid a necklace of cornflowers
Celebrate your donkey life

There are words too generous
to stay pinned to the page

String them like paper lanterns
among the Sycamores and
down in the subways

Set a Jester's Day
Wear cap and bells
Tell the truth till three o'clock

Listen till you hear the longing
underneath the rage

Don't leave the table

Tikkun Olam

At a concert in Jerusalem
Leonard Cohen stopped
in the middle of a song
and walked off stage

His offering was not good enough

In despair in his dressing room he heard
singing
The audience — a thousand voices
sang to him in Hebrew *Shalom Aleichem*
sang him back
He played *Marianne*, tears falling
The band cried, the audience cried

Who will sing you back?

A man is about to jump from
the high window, tell him
about the Redwood tree waiting to speak
with him for two thousand years

Sing him back

Cut one-inch strips of paper from
your notebook. Write:
You don't know how
important you are
to all of us
Write in Spanish, write in Chinese
tuck the message in people's grocery bags

Hear
the plea
in the horn of an eighteen-wheeler
to repair the face of God

Great Lord of Song
May we sing each other back

Dictionary Deity

Listen my beloved
in your worn leather coat
quiescent on the altar

Sovereign of all sentences
centurion of syntax
you serve the palaced and
the paupered just the same

Rich as an Everest of emeralds
the jeweled breath of Arcturus

But silent — ever silent

What if you spoke
to the mutilated world

Do we disappoint you
Squander your treasure
Speak but not with kindness

Make haste my beloved
Make the heart spacious
Release those words that heal

Twenty-six magic ships
at anchor in your harbor
twenty-six galleons of grace

Sail us to the truth

Tongue

My tongue carves minarets
in cream, a waffle cone
held in my happy hand

a melting grail

A famished deer licks
the salt that saves him

My dog licks my face
fifty sonnets worth

Thank you patient Holstein
Praise bean of vanilla

Society allows this public ecstasy
You can do it at noon
in front of the Prime Minister

First Flute

A Neanderthal man blows
into a dry bone
What he hears
makes him fall to the ground

A Manhattan man slips
his silver flute into his backpack
pulls on the sweater they gave
him at the shelter and goes
home

Down where indentured dragons
roar
down to the subway's platform
his wide front porch where he minds
his family
coming and going at all hours

Amid the drifting smells
of popcorn and cologne
he bathes the crowd in ballads
and blesses with the blues

He squints against the brilliant light
of his good fortune
If it weren't for that bone flute
he'd have nothing to give

Nobody should travel alone

without a song

Armies of The Rain

I curl up on long grass
drape my arm around the friendly shoulder
of your cemetery granite

I brought your old notebook
Words aren't flesh and blood exactly
but less and more
their ineluctable itch for epiphany

Here's page thirteen
We drove through midnight in Montana
I wrote down what you said
Wide strips of moonlight bandaged
that wounded barn

The moon is a nurse, you said

Words loved you
I mean they clustered around you
landing on your shoulders
like birds on St Francis

You found kindness everywhere

You said, Embrace the beggar in yourself
find a ruby in your pocket
Starlight spangles the grasshopper's eyes

I loved that
One Friday when I can no longer visit
We'll enlist in the armies of the rain

Spells

Much have I traveled in the realms
of gold. That's a spell
Do the hooves of the stallion glitter
the grass? Is there iridescent rain?

From a Grecian urn Keats heard
Truth is beauty, beauty truth
that is all ye know on earth

Wear that as a sash, a scarf
The Dawn's shawl. The archers
on the towers of mendacity forget
their purpose and drop
their arrows

Let words light on your shoulders
like the birds of Saint Francis
truth is beauty

I know the evenings empire returned
into sand

foster child of silence and slow time
or
Honored among wagons I was prince
of the Apple towns

before beauty, mendacity stumbles
suffers, retreats
and may
someday
bow

The Poet Contemplates His Wastebasket

All over the village
words weep in wastebaskets
asking
Where did we go wrong

Unread soon dead

Oh crushed paper peonies
crumpled chrysanthemums
shamed in crowded bins

You're not alone

Dear crinkly bouquets
of the damned, may you meet
in Second Chance Saloons
where clichés wear crowns
and adverbs get drinks
on the house

May you be tacked on the porch
With Tibetan flags
and fly out to the world
like prayers

Let Everything Happen To You. . .*

Six o'clock, Fifth and Market
A man lies crushed on the crosswalk

Blood, like a shawl, wraps his shoulders
and chest. The car that hit him kept going

A policeman stops traffic, sirens
scythe the air

I break from the crowd, calling
Sweetheart and kneel
beside him, take his hand
in my own. I kiss his brow

I've come to take you home
The ancestors gather among
the lilies by the river
Your place at the table set
with silver

I've never seen the man before

The sun swept up the shadows
to celebrate you today

Children play tag in the Orchard
It smells like cider and honey
Sheep on the hill quit grazing
to greet you

The bell in the courtyard rings
and rings, your dog with the star
on her forehead waits

The policeman crosses himself
reaches down, touches my shoulder

He's your brother?

Yes. I say. *He is my brother*

Raina Maria Rilke, Letters To A Young Poet

Whose Coat Is This?

Whose coat is this
with round of lace at the wrist
pockets proud with poems
Is it Percy Shelly's coat? Or Keats'?

Whose boots are these, stitched
in Spain but caked with good Irish mud?

Whitman's lilacs shake their perfume
on the cushions of Rumi and Shams
And Blake's tyger's blazing gaze
Did he who made the lamb make thee?

In a fancy of firelight I read
Goethe to Einstein in perfect German

Oh, the apple-breath of his pipe

I'll sing the camino in shackles of light

Leave the pocked polluted street
Enter the temple whose doors never close
Where no desire is denied, and no lie can delude
in the sky-windowed Temple of Solitude

Walking Without a Dog

I do not have my dog this year
so I've taken to the Grand Ideas
for my best company

They behave the same in many ways

The Idea bounds ahead of me
then races back and circles
crowned in golden burrs

One should touch the earth, said Rilke
like the first man

Worn soles learn the shapes of
stones, the suck of mud
My bare feet will part the grass
scrape coarse lichen

And we will walk, Rilke and I
through cherry blossoms and
falling snow

Past the delta, past the dunes
dropping the garments of thought

until it's awe and nothing else

Like the first man

About the Author

Rayne O'Brian lives north of the Golden Gate Bridge in a yellow Victorian with her two long-haired dictionaries.

Living on a Song a Day is her debut collection of poems.

www.ingramcontent.com/pod-product-compliance
Lightning Source LLC
Chambersburg PA
CBHW021916040426
42447CB00007B/893